C000185665

Supervision Skills

30127080472785

Supervision Skills

Supervision Skills

This workbook is written for and aimed at Managers and Supervisors or senior staff who wish to become Supervisors.

Supervision Skills has been devised to equip managers and senior staff with the knowledge and skills to enable them to provide supervision meetings in the workplace.

This interactive open learning workbook is filled with exercises and information on the responsibilities and the skills of the supervisor, the aims and benefits of supervision, styles of supervision, learning skills, ways to reflect and much more.

Suffolk Libraries	
DON	09/15
658.302			

First published in 2015 by SPC Publishing UK

Copyright © Suzan Collins 2015

All rights reserved. No part of this publication may be reproduced, stored in a retrieval system, or transmitted in any form or by any means, without the prior consent of the author, nor be otherwise circulated in any form of binding or cover other than that in which it is published and without a similar condition being imposed on the subsequent purchaser.

British Library Cataloguing in Publication Data.
A CIP catalogue record for this book is available from the British Library.

ISBN-13: 978-0-9931690-0-7

Acknowledgements:

The author wishes to extend her thanks to the following people for their contribution and support:

Andrew Williams, Home Manager
Anne Earley, Assistant Home Leader
Janet Elliott, Social Worker
Mary Purtill, Compliance and Regulation Manager
Tania Moore, Home Manager

Edited by: Jo Wilde
Book illustrations: Lynne Rooney
Cover creation: Jen Moon

Chinese proverb (p69) all reasonable efforts to trace the copyright holder have been made, and any queries should be addressed to the publisher.

Website addresses

The author has listed website addresses towards the rear of this workbook which were up to date at the time of writing.

©SuzanCollins2015

Contents   **Page**

Introduction 8
Why has this book been provided? 8
Who is it for? 8
How can this workbook be used? 8
Self-evaluation 11

Chapter 1 Responsibilities: Induction and Supervision 13
Manager responsibilities 13
Supervisor responsibilities 14
Supervisee/Worker responsibilities 14

Chapter 2 Supervision 18
Background to supervision 18
What is supervision? 18
Brief overview of process 19
Aims of supervision 21
The purpose and importance of supervision 21
Who can become a supervisor? 23
Goals and setting objectives 24
The benefits of supervision 29

Chapter 3 Supervision Practicalities 32
Frequency of supervision meetings 32
Time 33
Venue 33
Setting the scene 33
When to inform the employee that they will be having a
supervision meeting 34

Chapter 4 Styles of supervision meeting 35
Formal and planned 35
Informal and unplanned/adhoc 35
Face to face 36
Telephone or Skype 36
Specialist supervision 36
Peer group supervision 36
Group supervision 36
Three way supervision 37
Clinical supervisions 37

Chapter 5 Equality and diversity   38
The four main functions of supervision   38

Chapter 6 Preparing for a supervision meeting   40
What to do before the planned supervision   40
What to take with you   40
Setting the agenda   40

Chapter 7 Learning   42
Learning skills   42
Identifying learning styles   46
Different learning needs   47
Learning cycle   48

Chapter 8 Reflection   49
Reflective Practice   49
Reflective cycle   50
Time for you to reflect   52
Self-appraisal   53
Other ways to reflect   54
Continual Personal Development   54

Chapter 9 Supervisors   56
Skills of the supervisor   56
Listening   60
Body language   63
Feedback   65
Delegation   69
Motivation   69
Adapting to the needs of individual employees   73
Disagreements   77
Conflict   78

Chapter 10 Poor performance   80
Informal action   81
Formal action   82
Managing poor performance and/or absences   82

Chapter 11 Recording & Confidentiality ... 84

Supervision records ... 84
Responsibility for the safekeeping of the supervision records ... 84
Recording supervision ... 84
Keeping records ... 85
Which records to use ... 86
Confidentiality ... 87

Chapter 12 Final points of Supervision ... 89

Summarise the discussion and action points ... 89
Last supervision ... 89
Exit interviews ... 89
Exercises ... 90
Quiz ... 93
Self-evaluation ... 104

Appendices

1. Supervision Agreement ... 106
2. Personal Development Plan ... 108
3. Brief to help you, the supervisor get the most from
supervision meetings ... 110
4. Brief to help the supervisee get the most from their
supervision meetings ... 113
5. Supervisee Feedback Form ... 115
6. Supervision Form ... 117
7. Supervision Progress Form ... 120
8. Continual Professional Development Record ... 121
9. Certificate ... 122

Useful websites ... 124

References and Further reading ... 126

About the author ... 128

Introduction

Supervision Skills has been devised to equip managers and senior staff with the knowledge and skills to enable them to provide supervision meetings in the workplace.

Some organisations call supervision meetings a 'one to one meeting', or a 'support session'. In this workbook I will refer to it as a 'supervision' or 'supervision meeting'.

This workbook will provide guidance on how supervision is to be delivered to staff and explains the processes and requirements for supervision. Your organisation will probably also have their own policies and procedures in place for you to follow.

It is also a valuable source of guidance for any social care worker needing to learn or improve their supervision skills.

It is not always possible for staff to be taken off the rota to attend a training course and as a result this training workbook has been devised.

This workbook has a variety of training methods in it, including

- Reading passages where you will expand your knowledge
- Completing exercises
- Completing a self-evaluation which demonstrates the knowledge you have acquired.

This workbook has been written, first and foremost, to improve best practice and to enable staff to complete supervision training. If you are thinking about or working towards a management qualification you will find this workbook will be of great help to you.

This workbook is also suitable for people who like to learn at their own pace.

Towards the end of the workbook you will be asked to complete a self-evaluation on what you have learnt from completing this workbook. Once you have completed this your manager or trainer will complete the certificate on page 122 and give it to you. You will then have completed training on 'Supervision Skills'.

I hope that you find this a useful workbook and wish you well in your career. This workbook can be:

- Read from front to back
- Used as a reference book where you can dip in for information.

When referring to the people you support I have used the words 'individual' or s/he'.

Name of Learner (Your name) ....

Signature of Learner ....

Date ....

Name of Manager/Deputy Manager/Trainer ....

.... Date ....

Signature of Manager/Deputy Manager/Trainer........................

.... Date ....

Workplace address

....

....

Before you start this workbook here are two questions for you to consider

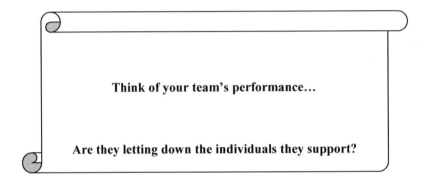

Think of your team's performance...

Are they letting down the individuals they support?

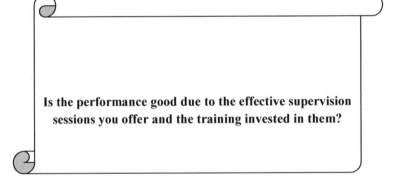

Is the performance good due to the effective supervision sessions you offer and the training invested in them?

 Self-evaluation

This exercise is for you to evaluate how you initially perceive your skills in supervising staff. Nearing the end of the workbook you will be asked to complete it again and compare your scores.

Score yourself between 0-10

10 = I know everything about supervision; I am perfect at delivering supervision

0 = I am new to supervision and know nothing in this area.

Understand the responsibilities of the supervisor and the supervisee	0 1 2 3 4 5 6 7 8 9 10
Understand what supervisions are	0 1 2 3 4 5 6 7 8 9 10
Explain the supervision process	0 1 2 3 4 5 6 7 8 9 10
Create a safe environment for supervision	0 1 2 3 4 5 6 7 8 9 10
Understand confidentiality	0 1 2 3 4 5 6 7 8 9 10
Explain confidentiality to supervisees	0 1 2 3 4 5 6 7 8 9 10
Draw together the four elements of supervision	0 1 2 3 4 5 6 7 8 9 10
Plan an agenda	0 1 2 3 4 5 6 7 8 9 10
Problem solving	0 1 2 3 4 5 6 7 8 9 10
Work with difficult/reluctant staff	0 1 2 3 4 5 6 7 8 9 10
Identify learning skills	0 1 2 3 4 5 6 7 8 9 10
Possess listening skills	0 1 2 3 4 5 6 7 8 9 10
Give feedback	0 1 2 3 4 5 6 7 8 9 10
Organise and prioritise objectives	0 1 2 3 4 5 6 7 8 9 10
Use Supervision Agreements	0 1 2 3 4 5 6 7 8 9 10

Supervision Skills

Establish and maintain boundaries   0 1 2 3 4 5 6 7 8 9 10

Identify and write clear supervision

notes with goals   0 1 2 3 4 5 6 7 8 9 10

Understand the purpose and

importance of supervision   0 1 2 3 4 5 6 7 8 9 10

Discuss issues of diversity and equality   0 1 2 3 4 5 6 7 8 9 10

Understand equal opportunities in

supervision   0 1 2 3 4 5 6 7 8 9 10

Chapter 1

Responsibilities

Everyone who is supporting a person in the social care or health setting has responsibilities and it will depend on the position the person holds as to what their responsibilities are.

> **Supervision is a two-way process and both the Supervisor and Supervisee have responsibilities in ensuring the supervision is effective.**

Manager responsibilities

- Supervise staff or delegate this responsibility to a senior staff member

- Meet the supervision requirements as set out in your organisations' policies and procedures

- The supervisor must be able to receive and participate in own supervision

- Hold supervision meetings or delegate this task to a senior member of staff

- Ensure that staff who are/will be supervised have read the supervision policy or that they have had the process explained to them

- Ensure that Supervision Agreements are in place between each supervisor and supervisee and that these are reviewed at least once a year (Sample can be found on page 106)

- Ensure that supervision meetings cover support, accountability and development

- Act on issues from supervision meetings where appropriate

- Enable supervisees to reflect on their supervision skills

- Review and sample the completed supervision records at periodic intervals. The organisation's policy may state the frequency. If not, you could sample them every two months for senior staff who are new to supervising and approximately every six months for existing supervisors (unless you are unhappy about their work then you could sample more frequently).

Supervisor responsibilities (Many will be the same as the managers' responsibilities)

- Arrange and hold supervision meetings with those you are responsible for and for the agreed time and frequency stated in your workplace policies and procedures.

- Be a good role model and demonstrate good practice

- Ensure the staff being supervised understand what to expect from supervision meetings and what they can and cannot do within their job role

- Make the supervisee feel important. If the supervisee feels the supervision is just a meeting with his/her supervisor then the supervisions will not be effective

- Ensure the supervisee understands confidentiality, and that this includes not posting photographs or commenting about work on social networking sites i.e. Facebook, Twitter etc.

Supervisee/worker responsibilities

- Prepare for the supervision meetings by identifying issues to be discussed and areas that need reflection

- Make a list of issues to bring with them

- Attend and participate in supervision meetings

- Ask questions about work they are unsure about

- Implement actions agreed after the session

- Keep the contents of the supervision meeting and their own copy of their supervision record safe and confidential

- Learn from mistakes

- Share responsibility with the supervisor for making the supervision work

- Not to rely on the supervisor to find out things-share the pursuit of his/her development

- Understand what confidentiality means and that this includes not posting photographs or commenting about work on social networking sites i.e. Facebook, Twitter etc.

Workers have a responsibility for taking responsibility/initiative for their own Learning & Development and to improve their knowledge, skills, values and practice. Supervision meetings are one of the many ways a worker can show that s/he is working towards or has now met these.

As you can see both the supervisor and supervisee have responsibilities…'both to *ensure* that agency policy is implemented - which implies a controlling function - and a parallel responsibility to *enable* supervisees to work to the best of their ability. (Brown and Bourne 1995: 10)'.

Induction

Induction is a structured period of learning where new employees are integrated into the workplace within a specific timeframe.

The Induction period consists of receiving induction training and learning things in the work environment.

New staff must complete induction training and your Manager will be able to tell you what this entails.

How would you feel if you were a new employee and you were not given an induction period? Instead you were put on shift and expected to get to know the job as you went along.

....

....

....

How do you think the individuals receiving the service would be feeling?

....

....

....

How do you think the rest of the team on that shift would be feeling?

....

....

....

Does this happen at your workplace?   Yes/No

If you have answered 'yes' what can you do about this?

....

....

....

Skilled, dedicated and valued workforce

'The social care and social work workforce is the backbone of this country's care system. If we are to ensure that children and adults are looked after in a way that preserves their dignity and peace of mind, it is vital that we have a world class workforce that is skilled, dedicated and valued and supported to do its best'. (DoH, 2008)

This can be achieved by Managers providing a structured induction for the new employee and providing all employees with regular supervision.

Providing a structured induction for the new employee

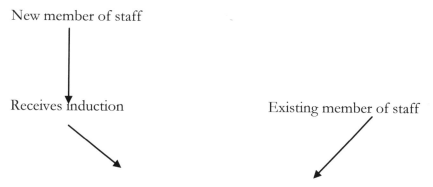

New member of staff

Receives induction   Existing member of staff

Participates and receives regular supervision meetings by senior staff who have been trained in facilitating supervision meetings.

Chapter 2
Supervision

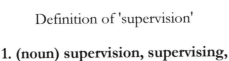

Definition of 'supervision'

1. (noun) supervision, supervising, superintendence, oversight
management by overseeing the performance or operation of a person or group

Background to supervision

There has been a tradition in social work, for example, for social workers to receive supervision and the first supervisors were experienced social workers who were employed in an organisation where both support and training was given. Fortunately the value and benefits of supervision have been widely recognised and it is used in adult health and social care and children's services.

What is supervision?

A process to guide, support and assist people who provide services to carry out their duties and assigned tasks, so as to achieve the planned outcome.

Supervision is key to helping staff in developing and maintaining the knowledge and competence to carry out their work.

Supervisors will encourage the staff they are supervising to:
• Assess their work and the effectiveness (reflect)
• Ask themselves-could I have done it better?
•Get information from individuals using the service, colleagues, families, other professionals.

Supervision is a continuous one to one cycle of experience where you reflect, analyse, plan, act and review.

Brief overview of process:

Member of staff.
(All staff in the care profession must receive supervision)

↓

Receives regular supervision

↓

Strengths, weaknesses and needs discussed (and training needs identified)

↓

Personal Development Plan devised

↓

Supervision meetings continue throughout the year, and include the Personal Development Plan (PDP) and the Continual Professional Development (CPD) form

↓

Annual Appraisal
An Annual Appraisal is a planned meeting between the person who holds responsibility for the employer and the employee which reflects on the past year and agrees objectives and Personal Development Plan for the forthcoming year. The supervision meetings will monitor the progress of these objectives.

Supervision is an important planned and structured meeting where one worker is given the responsibility by management to meet on a formal basis with another worker to develop his or her

Competence Knowledge Values Skills

and to meet objectives which can be organisational, professional and personal.

Not all of these will be given equal time or importance in every session as some will take priority over others. All areas will be visited over a period of time.

Personal Development Plan

A Personal Development Plan (PDP) is a plan devised between supervisor and supervisee based on aspirations, strengths, needs and competences. The plan will outline what to do to improve on agreed areas and when it will be completed by. (A sample of a PDP can be found in the appendices, page 108).

In the care sector we have what are called 'supervision meetings' which are linked to the annual appraisal where goals are set for the following year. The appraisal evaluates the worker's progress over a 12 month period and the supervision meetings monitor the working towards and completion of the goals. These goals are broken down into objectives and entered onto a Personal Development Plan (PDP) and this will grow and change as the individual progresses.

The supervision meeting is a formal planned meeting between an employee and someone in a higher position. This can be the manager or someone the manager delegates to, such as an assistant or deputy manager.

The supervision meetings identify organisational, professional and personal objectives and should include the needs of the people using the service

- organisation
- supervisee
- supervisor.

Aims of Supervision

- To identify strengths and areas of needs (weaknesses) and training needs
- To ensure staff carry out their duties effectively and in line with codes of practice/conduct and legislation
- To support the employee with their development
- To review workload and variety given and that the employee has the right tools and competency to do the job
- To support and provide encouragement for the supervisee
- To maintain and improve good practice
- To assist in the continuous professional development (CPD)
- To enable the employee to reflect on their practice.

The purpose and importance of supervision

I asked a manager this question...

Question:

What do you think the purpose of supervisions are?

Answer-

Supervisions are to fulfil the responsibilities of the employees post.

and I think this sums it up accurately.

A supervision meeting is an effective way:

- To listen to employees on a one to one basis and make the supervisee feel empowered
- To provide them with the necessary support and resources to undertake their role
- To provide mediation between the employer and the employee
- To set work objectives from one supervision meeting to the next.

Supervision is a fundamental part of the employee's learning and development:

- It is an important management function to ensure the supervisee has the relevant knowledge and skills and is accountable for practice and quality of service
- It enables the supervisee to reflect on their work practice, and their knowledge and understanding
- It reviews performance and identifies any problems or obstacles so they can be addressed. It is an opportunity for a confidential one to one. Staff want to do a good job and the employee will see that this time is for them to discuss and review their performance in a private setting
- It ensures that objectives, targets, tasks and standards remain relevant and achievable, and takes stock of progress towards objectives and performance against standards
- It allows agreement on future actions or support needed to move forward
- It builds the confidence of employees
- It confirms that the supervisee is doing the job correctly, enables staff to learn the role and grow by developing the skills required
- It allows development and training needs to be identified, such as the skills and knowledge needed to do the job.

> **If there are problems in relation to a supervisee's practice the supervisor must not try and change the supervisee's personality; it is the behaviour that needs changing.**

Supervision is a tool for:

a. development of performance
b. a key process of quality assurance
c. providing a skilled and professional work force

These supervision meetings are facilitated by a supervisor.

Who can be a supervisor?

A senior member of staff who holds the position of manager, deputy or senior can be considered for the role of a supervisor.

These supervision meetings are facilitated by a senior member of staff who has undergone training to become a supervisor and can

- support the individual to develop and plan their objectives
- arrange supervision meetings on a regular basis
- discuss an employee's performance at every supervision and at the end of their probationary period.

Probation reviews are sometimes completed during supervision meetings. Some organisations have a three month review with another review at the end of the employee's probationary period and some have it at the end of a six month period.

During the sessions the supervisor and supervisee will work through a supervisory form.

The aim of these sessions is to support the supervisee and to encourage reflective practice and development.

Annually, employees will receive an appraisal which can be done by the supervisor and/or manager.

The line manager will decide who will supervise whom.

Have a look at your organisation's policy. Does it tell you the frequency of supervision meetings employees should expect?   Y/N

If there is not a minimum or maximum number you will need to discuss this with your manager.

These supervision meetings provide an opportunity to:

- identify objectives to do the job more effectively and monitor the employee's progress towards these objectives
- provide support to meet these objectives
- discuss and monitor progress and day-to-day issues as they arise
- recognise progress and achievements
- discuss and identify training needs
- set goals and objectives which can be short, medium and long term.

Setting clear objectives

The goals that are identified should follow the S.M.A.R.T principles and be time limited.

Clear objectives can be set and measured by using S.M.A.R.T:

SMART is …
Specific   Measurable   Achievable   Relevant and realistic   Time bound.

Many organisations have their own design of personal development plans (PDPS). When breaking down the goals into objectives and entering them onto a personal development plan (PDP) please remember to use the S.M.A.R.T format.

Mary has been with you for two years. You have just taken her on as a supervisee as she did not get on with her supervisor. Mary gets on well with one client but tends to ignore the other clients living in the service. You hear from others it is because she does not know how to get on with them.

How do you tactfully tell her this?

………………………………………………………………………………

………………………………………………………………………………

Goals and objectives

Question-What is a goal?
Answer- A goal is a task that needs to be achieved. The goal is broken down into a set of objectives.

Setting the objectives
Question- Why do we set objectives?
Answer- To know what or how to do something to meet the goal

The scenario on the next page will give you the answer.

In your role of supervisor you have informed the supervisee called Mike that he needs to use sign language with Mr X (but Mike does not know sign language). You do not say anything else.

Question-

How does this make Mike feel with this limited information?

Answer-

Probably confused and lost as he does not know how to achieve the objective!

You need to set objectives to show Mike what he needs to do in order to meet the goals that were discussed and agreed with him.

They also need to be recorded so they can be measured. The scenario above cannot be measured. However, if you make it more specific to Mike in the supervision meeting he will know what to do to work towards meeting the objective.

A good example of using S.M.A.R.T to set and measure the objectives for Mike:

Specific	Measurable	Achievable	Realistic and relevant	Time bound
Mike will learn BSL sign language to enable him to communicate with Mr X	Attend training course	Yes	Yes	End of June 2015

Targets need to be clear. Employees will work towards them if they understand what is being asked of them.

S.M.A.R.T is setting up signposts to enable the supervisee to achieve.

©SuzanCollins2015   26

Supervision Skills

I met a senior support worker who was going through her probationary period and she said that she was really worried that morning when her manager suddenly announced, 'We'll have your supervision this morning' and walked away.

The staff member told me that she was worried in case she had done something wrong; she didn't have time to prepare and also wondered what time she would have the supervision.

Whilst she was on the telephone the manager put a note in front of her stating 'Supervision in 5 minutes, in my office.'

She said that in the meeting she listened to everything her manager wanted to tell her and then her manager gave her more work to do.

The manager then stood up and said, 'I will get the minutes typed and get you to sign them' and then walked out of the door.

There are many things wrong with the scenario you have just read. List at least three of them:

....

....

....

On another occasion I was discussing supervision training with a manager and he said he did not need to do supervisions as he sees his staff all the time. He tells them there and then what they have done wrong.

What do you think of this? How do you think the staff feel?

....

....

....

Another time when I was visiting a care home a staff member asked if I had five minutes and could we have a chat? Of course I said we could after the meeting I was there for. The staff member told me where I could find her later.

After my meeting I found the staff member and we went to a quiet area of the home. The staff member was quite reserved which was unusual for her so I knew something was wrong.

She asked me if she could tell me something and asked me not to tell anybody else. I said I could not decide this until she told me what it was, and if it was anything about harm to an individual I would need to report it.

She said that an individual had passed away whilst she was delivering personal care. He was very poorly and his passing on was expected. She went on to say she knew she had no right to be upset because she had only known him for a year, and other staff had known him for a lot longer. I was shocked to hear her express this, we discussed the situation. I told her, during that year I was certain she had provided care with dignity and respect to a high standard, and the resident would have known and appreciated her support.

As we talked more it became apparent that the manager had asked the majority of staff how they were feeling after the death but had not asked her. She again said 'I know I have no right but it was my first death…'

I advised her to ask the manager or deputy for some time to talk it through and she laughed… not in a happy way… I said perhaps she could ask for a supervision with her manager.

She went on to ask me if I knew what her supervisions were like and I replied that I didn't. She said that she received a form sent in the post to her home address asking if she has any problems, and to sign the form and put it back in the post. The form was her only supervision.

Identify two things that are wrong

....

....

The benefits of supervision

Supervision gives time to discuss the employee's development and focuses on the employee. It also clarifies the roles and the responsibilities they have.

...close parallel between the way employees are treated by their seniors, and the way the clients themselves are treated...if employees are supported and encouraged, they will take their own sense of well-being into their day-to-day work. (Kitwood 1997: 103).

Employees will be supported and informed of what they need to achieve and how to achieve it. It will praise the employees for things they have done well and will offer advice on how to do other things better, i.e. it will regularly evaluate their progress.

Supervision can be used to pass information from management to employee and this will result in the organisation being able to provide a better service delivery through the employee. This means that the people the employee supports will receive a better level of support and quality of life.

Training needs are identified.

Stress

It is said that a little stress is good for the body but too much could have a negative effect on the service the employee provides to the people s/he supports, to their colleagues and cause ill health to themselves.

Employers have a responsibility to be aware of work related stress, and to put things in place to reduce it.

Problems at work can be discussed and it is important that this is done because you, as their supervisor, need to know how your employee is feeling. By doing this you can help them when they are experiencing problems at work by looking at what can be done to reduce their stress levels.

A risk assessment on Stress may be needed.

Benefits for the individuals receiving the service

- Receive Person Centred Care and Support
- Trained staff who will learn new and/or better ways to do things
- Staff are keeping up to date with new developments.

Benefits for the organisation

- Supervisor focus on the supervisee
- Addresses good and poor performance~ regular evaluation of progress
- The supervisor can pass information from management to the supervisee
- The organisation will be able to provide a better service delivery through its employees. This means that the people you support will receive a better level of support and quality of life
- Staff commitment
- Staff retention.

Benefits for the employee being supervised

- A planned meeting on an individual basis
- It will encourage professional development
- It motivates the employee by spending time discussing his/her development
- Supervision is perceived as a safe environment where feelings can be addressed and problems and stress at work can be discussed and dissolved
- Staff are supported and informed of what they need to achieve and how to achieve it
- Increase in understanding
- Increase in confidence
- Addresses good and poor performance~ regular evaluation of progress
- Positive Feedback
- Supervisor focus on the supervisee
- Trained staff who will learn new and/or better ways to do things
- Keeping up to date with new developments
- Job satisfaction
- Benefits for the Supervisor
- Supervisor focus on the supervisee
- Addresses good and poor performance~ regular evaluation of progress
- The supervisor can pass information from management to the supervisee, including delegation of tasks
- The organisation will be able to provide a better service delivery through its employees. This means that the people you support will receive a better level of support and quality of life
- Staff feeling that they are supported is one way of retaining staff, which means there is a low turnover of staff which means individuals receive consistent support
- Employees are clear about their role
- Training needs are identified
- Goals are set.

Chapter 3
Supervision Practicalities

Frequency of supervision meetings

The frequency of supervision will depend on your work setting and your workplace policy and the experience of the supervisee.

More frequent supervision meetings may be required when the staff member:
- is new
- is going through their induction period
- may be overwhelmed by the complexity of the work
- needs extra support, e.g. may have been involved in an accident or incident or reported some alleged abuse
- is not meeting deadlines
- is persistently underperforming.

The supervisor and the staff member need to discuss this extra time otherwise the staff member could feel that s/he is being treated unfairly.

Part-time staff, Agency staff and temporary staff should receive supervision in the same way as permanent staff.

Supervision meetings normally take place during your paid working hours.

✍ Please check your organisation's policy on the frequency of supervision meetings.

Time

This can vary from organisation to organisation and the length of the meeting may be dictated by the issues on the agenda. An hour to an hour and a half should be sufficient and you can always carry over non urgent items to the next meeting.

Venue

Where the supervision meeting is held can vary depending on the workers role, where they are based, if the employee has a disability etc.

The sessions can be held:

- in your office (but will the supervisee feel intimidated being in there?)
- the care home where the employee works
- sometimes if you work a distance away from the employee you may decide to meet somewhere half way
- somewhere quiet
- a confidential place.

Setting the scene

The venue and environment is important. You will need to choose a room which is quiet and in a private area, and where mobile telephones are turned off unless the person you are supervising is On-Call!! Tell others you do not wish to be disturbed unless there is an emergency!

You will need to consider where to sit. You do not want to be too far away from the supervisee but equally you do not wish to be sitting on his/her lap. You may like a little table for both of you to rest on but please try and make sure it is not a big heavy desk as these can create a big barrier, unless, of course you both sit at one end of it.

Sitting like this does not allow interaction and eye contact.

You may like to sit where you can discreetly see a clock. You may have a watch on but it may not look good if you keep checking it.

You may wish for the chairs to be the same height. If there are only two and one is higher than the other then you may choose to sit on the higher one. Swivel chairs are not a good idea as they are not comfortable to sit on for long periods and the supervisee could become restless and start swivelling; equally, you could too!

When to inform the employee that they will be having a supervision meeting

At the commencement of employment it would be good to set the first date and then at the end of each meeting you will both agree the date for the next one.

It is advisable not to hold a supervision meeting on the day or day after the employee returns from holiday. S/he will need to catch up on what has happened during their absence.

Chapter 4
Styles of supervision meetings

There are many styles/types of meetings and here are a few examples:

Formal and planned

A formal supervision is a regular planned and recorded supervision meeting which is held on a private one to one basis between the supervisee and the supervisor.

Informal and unplanned/Ad-hoc

If you work regularly with the person you are supervising you will naturally have conversations and discussions on day to day work issues, and the supervisee may need to check things out. If decisions are made during this time you must make the supervisee aware that you will be recording this on the supervision record and the individuals care plan (if appropriate). You need to do this to ensure you have a continuous record. Some may feel it is not important to record but it is.

It is not good practice to replace formal and planned supervision meetings with unplanned, informal or ad-hoc meeting because:
- There will be no structure to the meeting as an agenda will not have been written
- The supervisor will have his/her agenda but the supervisee will not have been asked to contribute, therefore it could be seen as a controlling exercise and misuse of power
- It could be interrupted
- The supervisee could be criticised for not knowing up to date information as s/he did not have time to prepare.

Unplanned or informal/ad-hoc supervision can be very useful but should not replace the private and planned supervision meetings.

Can you think of an example when informal/ad-hoc supervision would need to be recorded and write your answer here?

....

....

Face to face

This is one of the familiar ways to have a supervision meeting.

Telephone or Skype

These can be used by senior managers who work a long distance away from the supervisee who is in a senior/managerial position. Many sessions can be carried out on the telephone or by video (Skype). However, the senior manager will do some face to face supervision meetings.

Specialist supervision

When someone needs supervision and advice in a specialised area of work specialist supervision will be required and this should be identified in the supervision agreement. This can include peer, group or clinical supervision.

Peer Group supervision

This can be an important function if carried out properly.

Group supervision

Some managers hold group supervisions if there is a group element to a task. It is also a good way to consider what human rights, equality and diversity means to team members.

Group supervision should be additional to individual supervision and should not replace the individual supervision meetings which the employee has a right to receive.

Three way supervision

Where staff receive supervision from someone other than their line manager there should be an annual three way meeting to ensure clear communication and that the objectives and outcomes are clear.

Clinical supervision

'A formal process for professional support and learning which enables individual practitioners to develop knowledge and competence, assume responsibility for their own practice and enhance consumer protection and safety of care in complex situations. It is central to the process of learning and to the scope of the expansion of practice and should be seen as a means of encouraging self-assessment, analytical and reflective skill' (DoH 1993).

Clinical Supervision relates to staff working in health.

Chapter 5
Equality and diversity

Supervision sessions will provide the supervisor with opportunities to model behaviours which explore human rights issues, ensure equality and promote diversity.

Supervisors need to respond to the different needs of the staff they will be/are supervising.

All staff should receive induction and supervision and be encouraged to develop skills and knowledge irrespective of culture, religion, disability, sex, sexual orientation, race, age and amount of hours worked. Supervision notes will reflect that these issues are addressed.

Organisational policies may differ slightly in the functions of supervision. To give you an idea of what some of the functions could be I have chosen four functions of supervision.

FOUR FUNCTIONS OF SUPERVISION

Management of Performance
Learning and Development
Support and Negotiation
Mediation

Management of Performance

Understanding job description, responsibilities and the boundaries of the role
Understanding legislation, policies and procedures
Delegate responsibilities
Review responsibilities
Ensuring a job is understood
Care plans
Observation of employees
Monitoring the workload
Setting goals and achieving them
Appraisal.

Learning and Development

Help to identify learning styles and learning needs
Identify training needs and learning opportunities
Learn about their role, reflect and learn how to do things differently and better if needed
Give positive and constructive feedback
Promotion/qualifications if required by the organisation.

Support and Negotiation

Create a supportive environment where the supervisee feels confident to speak and the supervisor and supervisee have a trust in each other
Workload
Positive and Constructive feedback
Stress levels
Any worries
Lacking confidence or too confident
Monitor supervisee's health and refer to occupational health if needed
Discuss difference between support and counselling
Relationships with individuals being supported and staff and families where appropriate.

Mediation

Deal competently and sensitively with staff complaints
Brief staff on organisational areas
Represent staff issues to senior management.

All these areas need to be covered during induction and in supervision meetings but not necessary all areas need to be covered at the same time. When you start induction and supervision you will concentrate on the job description but as the individual grows in their role you will then be including other areas (as above).

Chapter 6
Preparing for a supervision meeting

What to do before the planned supervision

- Read through previous supervision notes
- Reflect on employees progress, achievements and performance in working towards and/or meeting objectives
- Think about any problems/obstacles that may affect performance, what can be put in place to reduce these, does the employee understand the policies and procedures, for example?
- Obtain feedback from colleagues (other managers and seniors)
- Start planning the agenda.

What to take with you

- previous supervision notes
- note pad and pen
- information on areas you wish to discuss
- information on the goals you will be setting
- job description (if supervising new employee for the first time)
- glass of water.

Setting the agenda

Supervision is a two way process and both the supervisee and supervisor must participate in making it an effective supervision meeting and one way to do this is for both people to make a list of what they would like to be discussed in the meeting.

You need to encourage supervisees to engage with supervision and take responsibility for working towards and meeting *their* goals. This will also include participating in setting the agenda. Some organisations encourage supervisors to have a standard agenda to ensure that the main areas are covered.

Areas on the standard agenda could be:

- Actions from last supervision meeting
- Health and Safety
- Reflection on incidents, risk assessments, work practices
- Key working
- Continuing professional development
- Refresher sessions on policies and procedures
- Sickness and well-being
- Attendance (including sickness and absence)
- Annual leave/TOIL (time off in lieu)
- Time keeping
- Caseload/workload generally
- Discussion on projects
- Training and development needs
- Professional relationships
- Overall employee performance
- Other issues e.g. for managers/senior staff
- Date and place of next supervision meeting.

On the agenda you can also have 'How are you?' and discuss areas that link directly or indirectly to work. Asking this question can be a thoughtful one but be careful that the supervisee does not tell you all their personal problems. You may wish to make it clear that it is work specific when devising the agenda.

If your organisation does not use standard agendas you can jointly agree an agenda with your supervisee using previous supervision records and noting issues that need to be raised. Areas on the agenda should include subjects relating to the supervisee's role and development.

TIP! Aromas - Be careful not to overpower/invade the room with perfume/aftershave. This could give the person you are supervising a headache.

Chapter 7
Learning

Knowing how the employee learns best is crucial. We all have different preferences and no two supervisees will be the same, e.g. one may feel comfortable being asked questions and the other may feel uncomfortable if you did this.

LEARNING SKILLS
The process of learning

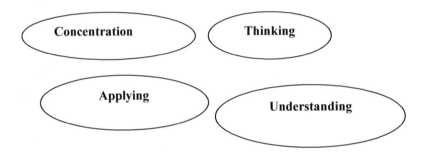

COACHING

Coaching is important in developing staff. You should identify opportunities and give guidance and feedback appropriately. There may be someone in the staff team other than yourself who can provide this coaching.

There may be times when you let the staff reflect on what they have done and there may be times when you need to intervene if the task is going wrong.

Remember the individual's strengths (no matter how small) and build on them.

Devise a coaching plan with review dates.

BAD=Brief, Action, De-brief

BRIEF:
The learner needs to have all the information needed to complete the task and asks self 'Do I see any problems? What are they?'

People are not born with learning skills, they have to develop them.

You have been on a training course where you were taught different ways to communicate with the people you support. When you are next at work you look forward to using some of the ways to communicate with Joe who has no verbal communication.

How would you know if you were communicating in the way that Joe preferred?

....

....

....

We learn something new every day, sometimes without realising that we are learning. However, some people say you need to go on a course to learn.

Think about something you learnt yesterday at work that did not involve going on a training course and write it here.

....

....

....

Here are some examples:

- An individual told you that she is now going to be a vegetarian
- Another individual told you that he wants to stop having toast for breakfast as the crumbs stick in his throat and wants to have cereal instead
- You read an updated care plan and found that the individual now wishes to have a lay in on a Sunday
- You read a risk assessment that showed you how you should support an individual to cross a busy road.

How do you learn best?

Knowing this is crucial. Not everyone stops to think about how they learn best. Attending a training course for some will meet their needs, for others they will need other ways to learn. The time of learning can have an impact on learning e.g. some people may learn better:

- during the day
- the morning
- the afternoon
- evening
- before meals
- after meals
- night

Here is an exercise you may like to ask the employee to do:

Observe the time you read a newspaper or magazine at home or a policy at work and if you absorbed/retained what you had read. If you have not then the time you read it was not your 'best time' to learn. You may wish to try this exercise a few times to find out which is your best time.

Learning styles

We all learn differently, for example some learn by:

- watching others who are more experienced
- reading literature e.g. journals, articles
- going to the library
- attending training courses
- searching the internet for information
- discussions in groups, team meetings, supervision meetings
- shadowing
- coaching
- mentoring
- role play (the word 'role play' can set alarm bells ringing to some people as they know they will be required to 'act out' something and for someone who is not confident they will not like this. Instead you could use the word 'simulation'.)

It will be beneficial for the employee to identify their learning style as soon as they can as the employee will find learning a lot easier. If they do not do this it could hinder them reaching their goals. For example if they learn best by watching others then you could arrange the opportunity for them to shadow another person with those skills, rather than read a book about it.

Identifying learning styles

There are a variety of learning style questionnaires around, on CD-Rom, paper copies, websites etc and here are two that I have used in the past for myself and with individual employees:

1. The V.A.R.K. questionnaire, i.e. Visual, Aural, Reading, Kinesthetic.
2. Honey and Mumford learning styles questionnaire i.e. Reflectors, Theorists, Activists and Pragmatists

1. The V.A.R.K. questionnaire 'V.A.R.K.'

Visual. Learns by looking at things, e.g. charts, maps, diagrams
Aural. Learns by sitting back and listening, e.g. talking things through, group discussions, lecturer
Reading. Learns by words e.g. reading and/or writing
Kinesthetic. Learns by watching others, being involved in the task/activity
More information can be obtained from http://www.vark-learn.com

2. Honey and Mumford learning styles questionnaire i.e. Activist, Reflector, Theorist, and Pragmatist.

Activist. Learns by encountering new problems and experiences, welcomes challenges and loves to 'have a go' and thrive in short term crises
Reflector. Likes to stand back and observe and do not like to be put under pressure, or have tight deadlines
Theorist. People like to be stretched intellectually and they like theory, systems, concepts and models
Pragmatist. People are practical and down to earth who focus on implementing and getting a result. There has to be a link between the subject and the employee's role and they also enjoy problem solving.
More information can be obtained from
http://www.peterhoney.com/content/LearningStylesQuestionnaire.html

Do you know your learning style?   Yes/No

If you have answered 'no' you may wish to complete one of the questionnaires.

Different learning needs

If the employee has a different learning need, e.g. difficulty in reading or writing, or English is not their first language; you (or the employee) can contact Learn Direct and arrange for a Word Skills check. This can be completed on a computer at a Learn Direct centre and will inform the employee about the difficulty they have e.g. with reading, writing, dyslexia etc.

Different learning needs can be: people with dyslexia, people who are deaf, have English as a second language, people with reading and/or writing difficulties, people who are visually impaired etc.

The employee may not wish to tell you if they have a different learning need but if they do not tell you then you cannot put things in place to help the employee. As the relationship grows the employee will begin to trust you and will feel comfortable telling you sensitive things like this.

> A person with a different learning need may need a different type of learning to that of conventionally taught training courses.

Following any training that has taken place the supervisor and supervisee should discuss and reflect on the training to ascertain if it has met the supervisee's needs.

Learning cycle

David Kolb, in 1984, developed a model to enable us to develop our practice which is called The Kolb Cycle. As you will see from the diagram below it has four stages. In order to learn, it is suggested that all four identifiable stages are completed in sequence and you can start at any stage.

In order to learn whilst doing something is not enough according to Kolb; we must also reflect on what we have done, draw on our knowledge and formulate concepts which can be used in new situations.

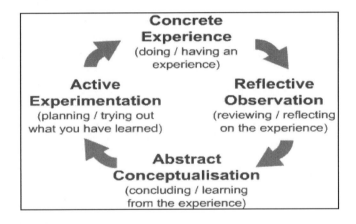

Chapter 8
Reflection

'A complex and deliberate process of thinking about and interpreting experience in order to learn from it'. Bond et al (1998)

As the supervisor you will help the employee reflect on their work. This will enable the employee to describe the situation and by explaining, it will enable the employee to sort things out.

Reflective Practice

A successful way of learning is to know what has worked well and what has not worked well in the past. It is good practice to encourage the employee to look at and evaluate what s/he has done as this will enable the employee to know if what s/he is doing is the most appropriate way to do something.

Discussion in groups at staff meetings or on training courses can be another way of reflecting. The employee discusses the topic and will hear others' points of view and this will enable the employee to develop and promote good practice.

Reflection can be uncomfortable for some people because you will be looking at what you have done (your practice) from a critical perspective.

Gibbs (1988) depicted reflection as a cycle. Something has to occur, then feelings and thoughts come (good and bad) and you evaluate the good and bad things that have happened. The next step is to think about what you have learnt from the occasion. You then look at how you could have done it differently and the final stage of this cycle is to think about what you would do if it happened again.

Reflective cycle

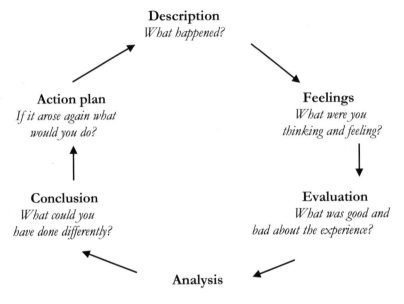

Description
What happened?

Action plan
*If it arose again what
would you do?*

Feelings
*What were you
thinking and feeling?*

Conclusion
*What could you
have done differently?*

Evaluation
*What was good and
bad about the experience?*

Analysis

What can you learn from what has happened?

Gibbs (1988)

Here is an exercise you may like to ask the employee to complete:

What I did recent...

....

....

What was I thinking and feeling? ....

....

What was good and bad about the experience? ....

....

What did I learn from what has happened? ....

....

What could I have done differently? ....

....

If it arose again what would I do? ....

....

Taking time to review work is beneficial and discussing it in supervision is all part of good reflective practice. As the supervisor you will want to see that the employee is taking some responsibility for their own learning and development and this will be one way to show this.

Time for you to reflect:

Our own experiences can shape how we do things. You may have experienced good and bad areas in your own supervision meetings with your supervisor. You will introduce the good into future supervisions that you facilitate but remember to leave out the bad! (You do not need to write your answers on this page if you do not wish to. Perhaps write them on a separate piece of paper).

What are your supervisor's qualities?

....

....

What are your supervisor's areas of need?

....

....

Which of your supervisor's skills will you introduce in the supervision meetings you will be facilitating?

....

....

Self-appraisal

If you have supervised employees before please list your strengths and weaknesses

Strengths

. . . .

. . . .

Weaknesses

. . . .

. . . .

Looking at your weaknesses, what are you going to do to turn these into strengths?

Weaknesses – What Will I do to make them into strengths?

. . . .

. . . .

. . . .

Other ways to reflect:
- Self-reflections
- Keeping a diary or journal
- Getting feedback from the individuals they support and/or colleagues
- Continuous professional development (CPD).

It is important for all staff to keep an up to date record of their continuous professional development.

CONTINUAL PROFESSIONAL DEVELOPMENT RECORD

Name ....

Covering the period from:

..............................to...........................

Date	What did you do?	What did you learn by doing this?	How have you/or will you use what you have learnt?	Any further action

©SuzanCollins2015

Case studies

Josie will be a new employee, she starts on Monday. What things will you put in place to ensure she is supported and developed as an employee?

....

....

....

Ian had his supervision six weeks ago and is due for his next one Tuesday week. What do you need to start doing?

....

....

....

It is Vicki's supervision at 11.30 this morning. It's now 11am. You have done all the preparation.

What do you do during the half hour before the supervision?

How do you feel: Nervous, anxious, happy, sad, rushed? *(Please circle)*

Explain your answer.

....

....

....

Chapter 9
Supervisor

Skills of the supervisor

 Have you supervised numerous employees?   Yes/No

If you have answered 'no' and are due to supervise your first employee then you may wish to run through what you will be discussing with your manager.

The supervisee will be exposing themselves to the supervisor and conflict can arise. There needs to be a professional relationship between the supervisor and supervisee and it is the supervisor's responsibility to ensure this happens. This can be achieved by building trust and the following can help:

- the supervisee having the same supervisor
- being reliable
- providing support
- keeping contents of supervision meetings confidential (unless they need to be shared e.g. in an investigation, disciplinary)
- treating the employee with dignity and respect
- knowing where to get information from
- knowing where to direct the supervisee to enable him/her to achieve his/her objectives
- helping with difficulties
- ensuring employee is being supported by colleagues
- ensuring the employee has learning opportunities
- if there are any action points that you are responsible for, then completing them when you say you will. If you do not complete them how can you expect the person you are supervising to complete theirs?

Have you experienced this (last situation) with your supervisor? Y/N
If you have answered 'yes' please explain how you felt

....

....

....

A supervisor should not supervise a relative as this can cause conflict of interest

Supervision meetings should be planned in advance and not held just when there is a problem.

Your supervisor has just come up to you and said 'We need a supervision, I have a free gap for the next half an hour, let's have it now.'

How would you feel? ....

Your answer may have included: what have I done wrong? feeling worried; after all, what is the rush?

You have not had time to plan for it and therefore will not be able to feedback on the objectives. The supervision could therefore be one sided i.e. the supervisor doing all the talking!

A Supervisor needs to be able to:

- Provide a structured approach at each supervision meeting
- Develop an effective supervisory relationship by using appropriate interpersonal skills
- Ask the right questions on the worker's roles and responsibilities to start a dialogue between you and the person you are supervising
- Have "people skills" to help the employees accomplish objectives
- Identify areas of development and how to meet them
- Delegate work to the employee
- Understand the dynamics of the organisation and keeps self up to date with changes in legislation and best practice and your organisations goals
- Provide support in many ways, for example, for your supervisee to develop, help with feelings if they impact on the employees work, link to counsellors, occupational health etc
- Observe your supervisee, is s/he improving/developing? If s/he is not and there are no changes in their practice as a result of their learning then you will need to identify the performance issues and act accordingly, i.e. follow policies and procedures on capability and/or disciplinary. More information about this can be found on pages 80-82
- Pass down information from management to supervisee.

The people you will be supervising are individual people and you will find that each person may require different things from you at different stages of their personal and professional development.

You do not need to know the answer to every question they ask, but knowing how to get the answer will help!

There will be times when planning how to meet the same objectives that another colleague is better to support the supervisee than you. This is okay, you facilitate supervisions and support the person you supervisee. You can share the load.

A supervisor needs to enable the supervisee to:

- Reflect on things they do well and things they need to improve on or learn
- Be accountable for their practice
- Give positive feedback
- Challenge in a constructive manner
- Identify areas that need to be addressed and address them in supervision meetings
- Encourage the supervisee to contribute to supervision meetings e.g. prepare, plan and participate and take shared responsibility for agreeing the action points and completing those they are responsible for.

The supervisor must be able to receive and participate in their own supervision.

A Supervisor needs to be able to say 'no'

If there are things that you need to inform the employee about and it is not pleasant or you know that you may have to say 'no' to some requests why not try practice saying 'no', perhaps at home in front of the mirror so you can see your body language as well.

It can be difficult to say a clear 'no'; some avoid saying it and string people along. A clear 'no' lets people know what you mean.

Remember you are saying 'no' to the request, not to the person!

There may also be times when an employee is going to ask for something that you cannot agree to. You may be able to give the employee an answer straight away or you may feel that you want time to consider it.

If it is the latter, you can say 'Let me think about it' and also give a date when you will get back to the employee and how e.g. email, verbally, letter etc.

If the answer is 'no' then you will need to be assertive and say this. If the employee continues to talk about what s/he wants, be firm; continue to say 'no'.

Focus on the supervisee.

Be punctual!

Listening

Supervision is a two way process. The supervisor and the supervisee need to listen to each other and give each other enough time to talk.

Use open ended questions as this requires giving more information. If you used closed questions e.g. 'Have you completed the objectives from your last supervision?' the answer will be 'yes' or 'no'. If you asked 'how did you get on with the objectives we set in your last supervision?' the person is likely to give you more information.

Active listening

'The process of attending carefully to what a speaker is saying, involving such techniques as accurately paraphrasing the speaker's remarks.' en.wiktionary.org/wiki/active_listening

Listening skills

Listening carefully will enable you to:

- Give time for the supervisee to tell you things
- Better understand what the supervisee is telling you
- Respond to questions and queries
- Find underlying meanings about what the supervisee is saying
- Summarise what is being said.

©SuzanCollins2015

How to listen

- Lean towards the supervisee when s/he is speaking
- Nod your head at appropriate times
- Ask questions when the supervisee has finished speaking
- Do not interrupt the supervisee
- Maintain eye contact (but do not stare)
- Do not fidget, sit still
- Try to relax
- Have open body language (i.e. not folded arms, try placing hands in your lap).

The quality of your answers will show whether you have been listening effectively!

Barriers to listening

- Interruptions i.e. telephone ringing, people knocking on the door wanting your attention
- Email being left on and it pings each time an email comes in and/or you catch out of the corner of your eye the message that comes up which gives you the first line of the message on that email
- Mobile phone left on silent and it vibrates when a message comes through
- English as a second language
- Accents
- Local sayings not understood properly
- Worry or fear
- Clock watching to get to the next meeting/work requirement
- Restrictions on time allowed.

Ask a family member or colleague to help you with this *listening* **exercise:**

The family member/colleague will tell you about a recent topic e.g. holiday, trip to the shops etc. for a few minutes. Your role is to listen without saying anything.

When s/he has finished talking you can feedback to him/her what you remember being said.

You can also ask him/her:
- how the person knew you were listening
- to comment on your body language e.g. did you give too little or too much eye contact, were your arms folded etc.

Body language can tell a lot about the way a person is feeling. When giving information to another person their facial expression will show if they are happy or not with what you are saying/doing.

Professor Albert Mehrabian's communications model

Professor Albert Mehrabian has pioneered the understanding of communications since the 1960s. He currently devotes his time to research, writing, and consulting as Professor Emeritus of Psychology, UCLA. Mehrabian's work featured strongly (mid-late 1900s) in establishing early understanding of body language and non-verbal communications.

Here is a precise (and necessarily detailed) representation of Mehrabian's findings than is typically cited or applied:

- 7% of message pertaining to feelings and attitudes is in the words that are spoken.

- 38% of message pertaining to feelings and attitudes is paralinguistic (the way that the words are said).

- 55% of message pertaining to feelings and attitudes is in facial expression.   Albert Mehrabian, source www.kaaj.com/psych

> **Body language, like posture and facial expression, can give clues to what the supervisee is telling you.**

Body language
Here are some examples of body language

Staring (without blinking)
Directly staring at a person, without blinking, can mean-
- that you are upset/angry/annoyed at him/her
- can show you're not even listening-like you've drifted off/day dreaming!

Giving eye contact
In English culture we are told to 'look at me when I am speaking to you' and therefore not to give eye contact can be interpreted as:

a. You are not talking to him/her
b. You have no respect for him/her.

When talking we need to:
- look into the person's eyes (they reveal so much). A person wearing sun glasses can put another person off talking to them due to them not seeing their eyes. This can lead people to being fearful or feeling scared.
- see the person's eyebrows move
- see the person's mouth and watch it move.

We can lose a lot of understanding if we are unable to see facial expressions.

However, some cultures are taught to show respect by not looking in the eyes when speaking. Instead they may look down as a sign of respect.

Some may see eye contact (especially prolonged eye contact) as threatening and/or confrontational. Rather than look into the eyes when talking you could look at the person's eyebrows.

The speaker will hold eye contact for about ten seconds. S/he will look away briefly and then re-establish eye contract. The listener maintains eye contact for longer.

Folded arms
This is called 'closed body language' and can be interpreted that:
    a. You are upset/angry/annoyed
    b. You don't really wish to communicate with this person.

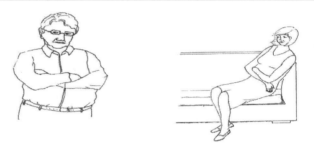

Legs crossed (with the leg nearest to the person crossed over the other leg)
Again, this is called 'closed body language.' By crossing your leg this way you are 'blocking' this person and your body is saying that you do not wish to communicate with him/her. Of course, it may be you are doing this without thinking; equally, the person you are supervising can do this without thinking.

Fiddling
This can convey that you are nervous or bored. If you don't know what to do with your hands place them on the table or in your lap.

Distance
You do not want to be too close to the person that you are supervising; equally you do not want to be too far away.

©SuzanCollins2015

Height

If you are sitting on chairs of different heights you need to choose the higher chair of the two. However, you should aim to get seats of the same height.

Voice

Your voice needs to be clear. Vary your tone.

Feedback

Having supervised numerous employees over many years I used to ask the employee how they felt they were doing before I gave my feedback, thus enabling the employee to assess their own performance.

You will need to provide useful and constructive feedback on the employee's performance and employees will be expecting this in their supervision meetings. The feedback needs to be:

Honesty	**Non-judgemental**
Clear	**Specific**

Honesty is very important and helps build up trust between the supervisor and supervisee.

Do not tell a supervisee that they are doing a good job if they are not. You may not want to tell the employee they are not doing very well but you have to. What will happen if the employee is not aware of their poor performance and it results in formal action being taken…e.g. capability or disciplinary procedure?

Constructive feedback is part of the learning process for the supervisee.

Remember you are giving feedback on the behaviour and not the personality of the person and you need to ensure the supervisee knows this is the case.

Give praise for work done well, and when needing to give feedback on things they have not done so well you can sandwich the news, e.g. start with a positive piece of feedback, then the negative and end with a positive.

Some people do not like hearing about things they do not do well as it makes them feel nervous, guilty or angry and aggressive.

Some people do not like giving feedback to others as it makes them nervous.

Feedback needs to be balanced and this can be achieved by using the sandwich effect, i.e. positive point, then a negative point then a positive point and so on.

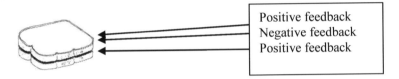

Positive feedback
Negative feedback
Positive feedback

Comment on good things as well as things that concern you; sandwich negative comments between two positive comments.

Employees cannot do a good job if you do not give clear feedback!

If someone has a very low self-esteem the supervisor will need to reinforce positive comments.

You need to review the feedback you have given to others in order to know if your feedback has been given in a positive manner and that the message received by the supervisee is the same message you gave.

Here are a few feedback exercises you may like to try

Ask a colleague to whom you have given **feedback** to write down the feedback they received from you.

Was the feedback received from you the same as you gave to the supervisee?   Yes/No

The amount of feedback required can be individual to each employee. Why not ask the supervisee if you are giving the level of feedback s/he requires? And if you are not, what more do they want you to give them?

You need to own the feedback e.g. when giving feedback use 'I' rather than 'someone thinks you are having difficulty with…'

Remember
- Feedback encourages development
- Positive feedback boosts self-esteem and motivation
- Performance can be improved if weaknesses can be identified and worked on together
- Paying attention to a worker's self-esteem is crucial when dealing with criticism
- Agreed action on improving performance enhances commitment and trust
- Establishing an atmosphere of confidence helps
- Be specific and focus on the behaviour that needs to change.

Feedback is important in a supervision meeting and the supervisee will be expecting it. However, you can give feedback at other times and in different formats e.g. verbally, in a letter, e-mail etc.

Think back to when you received positive feedback from your line manager. How did you feel?

....

....

....

Now think of a time when you received negative feedback. How did it make you feel?

....

....

....

What could that person giving you the negative feedback have done to make it easier to digest?

....

....

....

Delegation

Part of your role as a Supervisor will be to delegate work to the employee you are supervising. Some people don't like to delegate as they don't want to lose control or they may feel that the person they are delegating too may do the task wrong or not up to the standard they do it themselves.

"Give a person a fish and they'll eat for a day; teach them to fish and they'll eat for a lifetime."

Delegating to others can free up your time and also develop the employee but there are a few things you need to consider first:

- What are the person's strengths, have they the skills to do the task?
- Have they got room in their workload to do the task?
- Be clear on what you expect the employee to do
- Arrange regular feedback meetings and progress updates.

Motivation

Many employees are curious about how they are doing in their job role and are motivated towards self-appraisal and reflective process.

Question-
What happens if the employee is not motivated?

Answer-
Then you need to look at the other aspects of the person which you have learnt about them during your supervisory relationship

Positive reinforcement, satisfying the person's needs, treating people fairly and setting goals can motivate people and these can be discussed and achieved in the supervision meetings.

David Mcclelland's needs-based motivational model

As you will see, McClelland's theory on human motivation has three dominant needs and these needs will vary from one person to the next.

Motivational needs	Characteristics and attitudes
The need for achievement	Wants to advance in their career Seeks achievement and the achievement is more important than financial or material reward Gets satisfaction out of doing a good job Regular quantifiable feedback is important so they can monitor their performance Prefers to work with high achievers or to work alone Needs a sense of accomplishment Achieving the aim or task gives greater personal satisfaction than receiving praise or recognition These people will make things happen and get results "They demand too much of their staff because they prioritise achieving the goal above the many varied interests and needs of their people".
The need for power	Wants to organise others Needs to lead Needs to make an impact

The need for affiliation	Need to feel accepted by others
	Need for friendly relationships
	Needs to be liked
	Enjoys teamwork
	Is a team player
	Conform to the norms of the group

Which one are you?..

....

Adapting to the needs of the individual employees

Most supervision meetings run smoothly. However, you need to be aware that there may be times when they do not.

It may be beneficial to consider this as each person is an individual and you will need to adapt to this e.g. is the person confident, nervous, garrulous (talks too much- how will you get a word in?), likes to get the supervision over quickly and so agrees with everything you suggest, or will try and drag out the meeting because s/he likes the one to one time with you or by doing this avoids work.

Does the supervisee have a special need e.g. deaf and needs an interpreter?

Take some time and think of the employee you will/may be supervising.

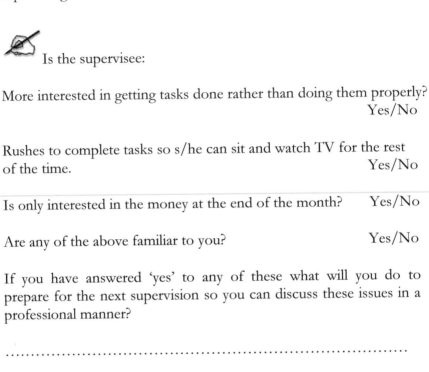 Is the supervisee:

More interested in getting tasks done rather than doing them properly?
Yes/No

Rushes to complete tasks so s/he can sit and watch TV for the rest of the time.
Yes/No

Is only interested in the money at the end of the month?   Yes/No

Are any of the above familiar to you?   Yes/No

If you have answered 'yes' to any of these what will you do to prepare for the next supervision so you can discuss these issues in a professional manner?

....

....

Employees will be at different levels to each other and therefore will expect different things from you.

Preparing for supervision and adapting your skills to meet the needs of each individual can enable a supervision meeting to run smoothly and productively!

Prepare!

How to deal with a range of behaviours that might be displayed in the meeting by the supervisee:

Employee new in post and new to supervision

This employee could be nervous and not know what to expect. You may wish to arrange for an existing employee who has received numerous supervisions to talk him/her through what happens. Of course, you can do this but sometimes it is better coming from a colleague who is at the same level as the employee.

Employee having a change of supervisor

Change of supervisor can happen after a request from either the supervisor or the supervisee. Where possible both people should discuss the reason why a change is necessary as honestly and diplomatically as they can. It is important to get it sorted now rather than at a later date when it is worse.

If you are the employee's new supervisor you will need to bring yourself up to date with the employee's previous supervision records and the previous supervisor should hand these over to you. Whilst you are allowed to see these records it would be common courtesy to inform the employee that you were going to do this.

If the employee had a good professional relationship with the previous supervisor then s/he may want you to be identical to him/her in terms of skills and delivery. This can be difficult but the employee will adapt to you, given time. You will both be starting out on a new professional relationship where trust needs to be built by both of you.

Employee has been in post for a long time

The employee may be feeling a little frustrated and in need of a new challenge. Frustration can be reduced by:

Giving this employee (depending on their knowledge, skills and values) responsibility, for example, inducting new employees.

Looking at the job description of the role above the workers current one and discuss with the employee how s/he can work towards these objectives so they can be in a position to apply for a higher position when it is advertised. You need to make it clear that the employee will not automatically get the post but will be in a position to apply for it once they have gained the necessary skills. This can be a good way of retaining staff.

Nervous employee

Employees can be nervous for a variety of reasons e.g. bad experiences in the past, always being told they have done things wrong, not being able to understand what is being asked of them (language barriers) etc. They may become so worried that they do not take in anything that is being said to them and do not contribute for fear of being told they are useless or they 'did it wrong again'. Or it could be that the employee is new to the care field and is finding it difficult to adjust.

In situations like this you may need to do some repair work on highlighting their strengths. You may also wish to have shorter supervision meetings i.e. have two separate half hour meetings rather than one whole hour.

You can acknowledge to yourself that the employee is nervous but do not let this rub off on you and make you nervous.

Employee wants more holiday

What would you do if an employee announced in their supervision today that although s/he had last week off, s/he wants next week off too, but was told they could not have it and became very upset and perhaps angry?

....

....

I guess your answer would be similar to some of these:

Recognise the upset or anger by saying 'I can see you are upset, let's sit and discuss it and see if we can work this out.'

Use your listening skills with regard to what the employee is telling you (not what you think they may be saying). S/he may have a very valid reason for wanting or needing the next week off. I guess you have noticed the difference between **wanting** and **needing** the next week off?

If s/he **wants** the next week off to go and visit friends then it is more than likely you would not want to give this week off (due to having to arrange staff cover and the inconvenience etc). This will have an effect on the team and you will need to be discussing teamwork and fairness within the team with the individual.

However, if s/he **needs** the next week off because his/her mum fell and broke her leg whilst the employee was on holiday last week and there is no one to look after her, then you may respond to this in a different way.

Employee who does not wish to be supervised

Every employee has a right to be supervised and organisational policy states every employee MUST receive supervision.

The reasons you may hear could be:

- Culturally the male employee does not want to be supervised by you if you are female or vice versa
- You both live in the same street and the supervisee does not feel comfortable with you having knowledge about him/her.
- The supervisee feels s/he is more knowledgeable than you
- The supervisee feels superior to you
- The supervisee may be finding it difficult to adjust to their new job or the additional responsibilities but does not want to tell you this
- Meeting with the supervisor means looking at what s/he has or has not done.

Can you think of any more reasons?

....

....

....

If the employee does not want to be supervised by anyone then this is an issue that needs to be discussed with the manager and Human Resources as this could lead to capability or disciplinary procedures because every employee in the care sector MUST receive supervision in line with his/her contract and job description.

A record should be made if the employee, for whatever reason, avoids or misses a supervision meeting due to sickness, lateness, being too busy or making excuses e.g. I forgot I had one, I haven't done the work, it's not important we can always rearrange etc.

If the person has been off work for a prolonged absence a 'return to work interview' will be held and the workplace should have a policy on this for you to read.

Disagreements

There may be times when you both disagree on an opinion. After discussing it if you both continue to disagree then say, 'We have spent a while debating this, lets agree to disagree' and record this on the supervision notes.'

If the supervisee was disagreeing with something factual relating to the people you support, e.g. not following a care plan, then you need to inform the employee that this is a written document and agreed by the person receiving the service and others and needs to be followed to ensure the meeting of needs and involves a consistent approach from staff. You could say to the employee that you will discuss it further with the manager but in the meantime s/he must follow the care plan.

If there is a disagreement between yourself and the employee, firstly try and sort it out between yourselves, If this does not work then the supervisor and the supervisee have the right to discuss it with the supervisor's line manager.

The Supervision Agreement should include how the supervisee can complain if the Supervision Agreement is not being met.

Complaints about the behaviour of the Supervisor or the Supervisee can also be taken to the Manager.

Not completing action points from supervision meetings

If the employee has not completed some of the action points from the last supervision meeting, you will need to discuss these with him/her in the supervision meeting.

There may be a valid reason, such as heavy workload or the needs of the person receiving the service has changed etc.

You can also discuss if the supervisee needs extra support and you both can set a new date on when the actions will be achieved by.

If there is not a valid reason you will need to explain the importance of completing these by an agreed date and the consequences of not completing them e.g. capability, disciplinary etc.

Standards of work

It is important for staff to know the standard of work is required. For example if you ask the employee to write an account of something or to devise a chart etc. please be sure to tell them how you would like it done. Do not assume that they will know.

Are all staff clear on the standard of work they should deliver? Yes/No

If you have answered 'no' what can you do about this?

Conflict

If an issue is not resolved or the supervisee has not completed their action points from the previous meeting and there is no reason for this, it can cause conflict.

Some signs of conflict can be

- Uncomfortable silences
- Employee avoids specific subjects
- Supervisor has to refer to policies and procedures
- Issues that have not been resolved are on the agenda again!

Some examples of the causes of conflict

- Not having the resources to do the task
- The supervisor thinks differently to the supervisee and vice versa
- The supervisor thinks negatively of the supervisee or vice versa and the person picks up on this
- Angry words/threats.

Some examples of how to minimise conflict

- Discuss ways on how the task can be achieved with the resources available
- We all think differently and having different opinions and ideas can enable you to think outside of the box
- It is very easy to pick up on what people think of us. If you think bad thoughts about the supervisee s/he will pick this up and will react thus causing conflict. Try and see the positive side of the person.

Serious conflict would be dealt with through mediation, usually with the Supervisor's manager.

Chapter 10
Poor performance

'Poor performance can result from role overload or unclear objectives or unrealistic targets. Changes to the work environment would probably raise the level of performance. On the other hand, absence (which can again be seen as a sign of poor performance) or a personal or a domestic problem, may be better handled by Occupational Health'. (Strebler, 2004)

Yawning

Poor performance must be looked at quickly and seriously because:

- If someone is not doing what they should be doing it can put the individuals and/or staff at risk
- Individuals may not be getting the service they deserve
- Other staff have to do that persons work as well as their own. They will become tired and stressed, and resentment could kick in.

It is important to look at why the employee is performing below the required standard, it may not be his/her fault. There are many things that can affect the performance of the supervisee, such as;

- Team dynamics-harassment, bullying, staff not pulling their weight etc.
- Lateness/timekeeping
- Problems at home, i.e. childcare, divorce, caring responsibilities.

Where possible try to support and work with the individual. For example, is the lateness due to the bus timetable changing, or the individual has caring responsibilities and cannot start his/her shift until one hour after it started? If it is, can the employee start a little later and finish a little later?

Deal with it now rather than later when it could get more serious!

INFORMAL ACTION (which can be dealt with in supervision meetings):

- Avoid being judgemental
- Support the employee to meet their objectives
- Ensure the employee knows what is expected of him/her and takes responsibility
- Give a time for the action points to be completed (improvement may not happen immediately)
- Provide training or for someone to go through the task with him/ her
- Ensure the employee knows the consequences if s/he does not improve
- Devise an action plan
- Monitor the employee's performance and give regular feedback on the practice that needs to be improved.

Your organisational policy should give guidance on how long this informal stage will be via supervision meetings.

Go and have a look at it now and write here how long the informal stage will be.

In my organisation the informal stage will be……………………..

The diagram shows a way of managing poor performance

Turning on the TAPS	
T	timely and early
A	appropriate management style and response
P	keep it private
S	make it specific to performance, and factual
Source: IES	

(Strebler, 2004)

Once the time length for the informal action has expired if there is no improvement you will then need to discuss this with your manager and/or Human Resources and consider whether formal action is required. It will depend on the position you hold as to whether you are involved in this or not. An overview of formal action can be found in the appendices.

FORMAL ACTION

Formal action will mean following the Capability, Disciplinary or Sickness/Absence Procedure and you will read more about this on the next page 82.

CAPABILITY PROCEDURE (problem with competence)

Is the employee capable of doing the job they are employed to do?

Some examples

Employee has tried to fulfil the objectives that were set in supervision meeting and areas on his/her job description but is unable to, despite having training, extra help etc.

DISCIPLINARY PROCEDURE (problem with conduct)

Some examples:

- Refusing to follow policies, procedures and regulations
- Disobeying instructions
- Refusing to work towards and meet the objectives as set out in his/her Personal Development Plan
- Absent from work without permission, abusive behaviour etc.

SICKNESS PROCEDURE (problem with their health)

Some examples:

- Short periods of illness which are frequent and each time there is a different reason
- Pattern of being off sick the day before and/or after a weekend off.

Capability, Disciplinary or Sickness/absence Procedures/Policies

If you do not have copies of the Capability, Disciplinary or Sickness/absence Procedures/Policies in your workplace you can find information on the internet, including on the ACAS website http://www.acas.org.uk

Chapter 11
Recording & Confidentiality

SUPERVISION RECORDS

- give a start point to the next supervision meeting
- are evidence that supervision has taken place
- summarise discussions and issues
- record discussions
- discuss and record the actions, including the timescales that have been agreed to complete these
- must be kept in a secure place.

Responsibility for the safekeeping of the supervision records

The supervisor holds the responsibility for the safekeeping of the supervision records. These records need to show a true reflection of the interaction between the supervisor and the supervisee.

Your workplace policy should tell you when the supervision notes need to be ready and given to the supervisee.

Recording supervision

Details of decisions made, the timescales for completion and who holds responsibility for these actions should be recorded in writing and the supervisor is responsible for recording the meetings. A summary of what was discussed and the action points arising/agreed should be recorded as a minimum.

Copies of the supervision notes must be signed and dated by both parties with a copy going to the supervisee and one to the supervisor.

Disagreements need to be recorded also, tactfully! And the supervisee should be able to add their comments to enable this to become part of the session.

The discussions need to be recorded and these recordings need to be factual, sensitive and professional, highlighting action points and progress made since the last supervision.

The recording will reduce any confusion or disputes.

The recording can be:

Written by hand (if you have clear hand writing) or typed.

Typed minutes can be safely stored on the computer and password used so no one else can see them.

If the supervision records are to be typed by someone other than the Supervisor then the supervisor must get permission from the Supervisee for this to happen, especially around issues of a personal or sensitive nature.

Some supervisors prefer to type the minutes of the supervision. It is important to print out copies and sign and date them, just in case at some point they are used in an investigation case. The hard copies prove that the records have not been tampered with.

Keeping records

The supervision records must be kept on the supervisee's file held by the supervisor, in a secure cabinet. Other documents can also be put in this file, such as the individual supervision agreement, copies of appraisals etc.

Many organisations keep supervision records for a period of two years.

If/when the employee leaves the organisation records should be archived and kept for two years after the supervisee has left the organisation. The records will then be destroyed.

Please check with your Manager if your organisation's policy is the same.

Which records to use

Your organisation's policy will inform you on which formats you can use and here are a few examples:

- Organisational forms that have individual headings
- Hand written
- Typed. These can be sent via email to the person's work email address. The supervisee will be asked to reply to the email to confirm they have received and agree the minutes of the supervision. (It is good practice to print out the minutes and for the supervisor and supervisee to have their own signed copies)
- Duplicate pads. These pads allow the supervisor to hand write the minutes and give a copy to the employee being supervised and one copy for the file.

A question I was asked when I delivered training on Supervision Skills…

Q: What kinds of words should I use to put on the supervision record? Do they have to be posh?

A: You should sum up each point and write it on the form. You should use everyday words that you and the supervisee can understand. They should be concise, to the point but detailed enough so that the issue, including the reason for any decisions taken, can be revisited at a later date and be understood.

Records may be used in any capability or disciplinary proceedings.

Under the Data Protection Act staff can access any records written about them and your organisation will have a policy on 'access to files'. The staff member wishing to access the information will need to contact their Data Protection Officer and if one is not in post then it is suggested that they discuss their wanting information with their manager or Human Resources. Whilst it says 'access to files' there may be occasions when information is withheld and there will be justifiable reasons for this.

Record in front of supervisee or not?

If you are writing, it will be difficult to engage in the conversation and you may miss important non-verbal communication. Perhaps make notes and write them up later?

Confidentiality

The contents of what was discussed and agreed in the supervision meeting and the records written are private between the supervisee and supervisor. The employee being supervised needs to know that these records belong to the organisation and therefore absolute confidentiality cannot be guaranteed as others may need to see them.

For example:

They may be reviewed for operational purposes e.g. to ascertain training needs

They may be required for a disciplinary hearing

The line manager (who may not be the supervisor) may wish to see them to ensure quality of supervision at periodic intervals.

Human Resources may need to see them if it has been revealed in a supervision meeting something that relates to abuse of an individual or an act of misconduct etc.

The Care Quality Commission.

The supervision notes held by the supervisor will be kept in a secure location and the supervisee will need to be informed to keep his/her copy safe too.

Supervision records are transferable and should go with the employee if they transfer to another service within the same organisation.

Have you shared something in confidence and that person has then told someone else?   Yes/No

If you have answered 'yes', how did you feel?

....

....

....

©SuzanCollins2015   88

Chapter 12
Final points of Supervision

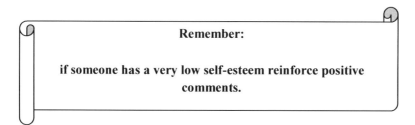

Remember:

if someone has a very low self-esteem reinforce positive comments.

SUMMARISE THE DISCUSSION AND ACTION POINTS

- Go through each item on the agenda and clarify what was agreed
- Ask questions to clarify if required
- Discuss how, when and by whom the objectives are going to be met
- Set dates on when the objectives and action points will be achieved
- Set date for next meeting
- Thank the supervisee for a good meeting and for achieving the previous goals etc.

LAST SUPERVISION

It is very important when an employee is leaving for him/her to have a supervision meeting. The last supervision is very important not only to wrap things up and arrange for tasks to be passed onto another staff member but also to give positive feedback on what the employee has done and to say 'Thank you'.

EXIT INTERVIEWS

Exit interviews take place when an employee is leaving the organisation and the aim is to identify why the employee is leaving and see if there are any trends on staff leaving. If there are any trends these can be addressed by the manager.

NEARLY THERE!

You have almost completed training on Supervision Skills.

In pairs please complete this simulation:

EXERCISE NO: 1

You are a supervisor and are now going into supervision with Mary. Mary has been with you for two years. In the supervision you will tell Mary how well she did in supporting the client to vacuum the dining room floor. You would like her to start working with the other clients too (you hear from others that she will not support others as she does not know how to).

What did you learn from doing that simulation?

....

....

....

How did you feel doing that simulation?

....

....

....

EXERCISE NO: 2

You are now going into supervision with Mark. Mark has piercing through his nose, lip and has numerous earrings in each ear. You will be discussing this with him in his supervision today as it is a health and safety risk.

What did you learn from doing that simulation?

....

....

....

How did you feel doing that simulation?

....

....

....

EXERCISE NO: 3

You are in supervision with Jane. Prior to the supervision a colleague came and informed you that Jane had not supported an individual to the toilet as she should have done; consequently the resident has been incontinent and is deeply distressed.

What did you learn from doing that simulation?........................

....

....

....

How did you feel doing that simulation?...........................

....

....

QUIZ

List two responsibilities the Manager has

1.

2.

List two responsibilities the Supervisor has

1.

2.

List two responsibilities the Supervisee/Worker has

1.

2.

What is supervision?

List two benefits of supervision for the supervisee

1.

2

List two benefits of supervision for the individual receiving the service

1.

2

TRUE/ FALSE EXERCISE

A supervision meeting should be between one and one and a half hours	True or False
More frequent supervision meetings may be required when the staff member is not meeting deadlines	True or False
Supervision meetings should take place outside of working hours	True or False
Supervision meetings should be held in a quiet, confidential place	True or False
Ideally chairs need to be the same height	True or False

STYLES OF SUPERVISION

```
P  L  S  Q  H  S  G  R  O  U  P  L  M  K  L
V  L  K  N  X  A  D  E  N  N  A  L  P  N  U
E  Y  A  Q  E  K  W  X  V  C  G  B  A  Y  P
L  X  S  N  E  X  M  C  I  C  F  E  S  Y  I
R  G  K  F  N  Q  P  N  R  O  E  U  C  S  G
R  E  E  P  N  E  I  N  R  W  P  P  Y  A  Y
B  N  I  Y  Q  L  D  M  T  E  E  T  Y  P  F
N  O  T  A  C  Q  A  F  R  C  D  U  D  K  Y
O  H  X  W  F  L  R  V  I  L  O  A  I  X  S
B  P  V  G  D  S  I  Y  B  C  G  W  B  N  P
Q  E  O  N  S  S  Q  R  S  Y  Z  W  Y  J  D
I  L  N  X  I  I  N  F  O  R  M  A  L  U  P
Q  E  T  O  N  G  Z  T  H  R  E  E  A  Z  Q
S  T  N  W  K  S  P  E  C  I  A  L  I  S  T
U  Q  X  H  G  R  H  J  N  I  M  N  Z  I  C
```

FORMAL	TELEPHONE	SUPERVISION
PLANNED	SKYPE	CLINICAL
INFORMAL	SPECIALIST	THREE
UNPLANNED	PEER	WAY
FACE	GROUP	

FUNCTIONS OF SUPERVISION
List two functions

1.

2.

PREPARING FOR A SUPERVISION MEETING
List two things you should do before the planned supervision

1.

2.

List two things you should take with you

1.

2.

SETTING THE AGENDA

List two things that could be on the standard agenda

1.

2.

LEARNING
The process of learning

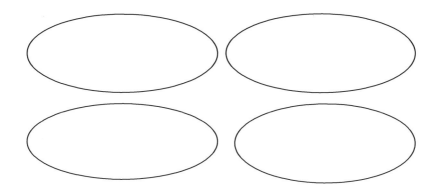

©SuzanCollins2015   97

LEARNING STYLES

List two learning styles

1.

2.

REFLECTION

Why is it important to encourage the person you are supervising to reflect?

SKILLS OF THE SUPERVISOR

List two skills of a supervisor

1.

2.

©SuzanCollins2015

LISTENING

List two barriers to listening

1.

2.

BODY LANGUAGE

WHAT do you interpret from the body language of these two individuals?

FEEDBACK
What is the sandwich effect?

POOR PERFORMANCE
Poor performance must be looked at quickly and seriously because:

SUPERVISION RECORDS
Why is it important to write supervision records?

FINAL POINTS OF SUPERVISION
Why is it important to summarise the discussion and action points?

Why are last supervisions important?

Why are exit interviews important?

SOLUTIONS:

QUIZ

List two responsibilities the Manager has (page 13)

List two responsibilities the Supervisor has (page 14)

List two responsibilities the Supervisee/Worker has (page 14)

What is supervision? (page 18)

List two benefits of supervision for the individual receiving the service (page 29)

List two benefits of supervision for the supervisee (page 29)

List two barriers to listening (page 60)

TRUE/ FALSE EXERCISE

A supervision meeting should be between one and one and a half hours	True
More frequent supervision meetings may be required when the staff member is not meeting deadlines	True
Supervision meetings should take place outside of working hours	False
Supervision meetings should be held in a quiet, confidential place	True
Ideally chairs need to be the same height	True

STYLES OF SUPERVISION

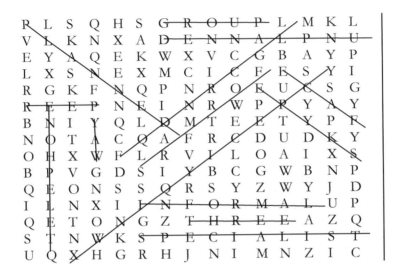

R	L	S	Q	H	S	G	R	O	U	P	L	M	K	L
V	L	K	N	X	A	D	E	N	N	A	L	P	N	U
E	Y	A	Q	E	K	W	X	V	C	G	B	A	Y	P
L	X	S	N	E	X	M	C	I	C	F	E	S	Y	I
R	G	K	F	N	Q	P	N	R	O	E	U	C	S	G
R	E	E	P	N	E	I	N	R	W	P	R	Y	A	Y
B	N	I	Y	Q	L	D	M	T	E	E	T	Y	P	F
N	O	T	A	C	Q	A	F	R	C	D	U	D	K	Y
O	H	X	W	F	L	R	V	I	L	O	A	I	X	S
B	P	V	G	D	S	I	Y	B	C	G	W	B	N	P
Q	E	O	N	S	S	Q	R	S	Y	Z	W	Y	J	D
I	L	N	X	I	I	N	F	O	R	M	A	L	U	P
Q	E	T	O	N	G	Z	T	H	R	E	E	A	Z	Q
S	T	N	W	K	S	P	E	C	I	A	L	I	S	T
U	Q	X	H	G	R	H	J	N	I	M	N	Z	I	C

FORMAL   TELEPHONE   SUPERVISION
PLANNED   SKYPE   CLINICAL
INFORMAL   SPECIALIST   THREE
UNPLANNED   PEER   WAY
FACE   GROUP

FUNCTIONS OF SUPERVISION
List two functions (page 38)

PREPARING FOR A SUPERVISION MEETING
List two things you should do before the planned supervision (page 40)

List two things you should take with you to supervision (page 40)

©SuzanCollins2015

SETTING THE AGENDA
List two things that could be on the standard agenda (page 40)

LEARNING
The process of learning (page 42)

LEARNING STYLES
We all learn differently, list two ways of learning (page 42)

REFLECTION
Why is it important to encourage the person you are supervising to reflect? (page 49)

SKILLS OF THE SUPERVISOR
List two skills (page 56)

BODY LANGUAGE
What do you interpret from the body language of the two individuals? (page 63)

FEEDBACK
What is the sandwich effect? (page 66)

POOR PERFORMANCE
Poor performance must be looked at quickly and seriously because (page 80)

SUPERVISION RECORDS
Why is it important to write supervision records? (page 84)

FINAL POINTS OF SUPERVISION
Why is it important to summarise the discussion and action points? (page 89)
Why are last supervisions important? (page 89)
Why are exit supervisions important? (page 89)

Self-evaluation

You will recall that at the beginning of this training you completed an exercise for you to evaluate how you perceive your skills. Now you have completed this training I would like you to complete it again and compare your answers.

Score yourself between 0-10

10 = I know everything about supervision; I am perfect at delivering supervision

0 = I am new to supervision and know nothing in this area.

Understand the responsibilities of the supervisor and the supervisee	0 1 2 3 4 5 6 7 8 9 10
Understand what supervisions are	0 1 2 3 4 5 6 7 8 9 10
Explain the supervision process	0 1 2 3 4 5 6 7 8 9 10
Create a safe environment for supervision	0 1 2 3 4 5 6 7 8 9 10
Understand confidentiality	0 1 2 3 4 5 6 7 8 9 10
Explain confidentiality to supervisees	0 1 2 3 4 5 6 7 8 9 10
Draw together the four elements of supervision	0 1 2 3 4 5 6 7 8 9 10
Plan an agenda	0 1 2 3 4 5 6 7 8 9 10
Problem solving	0 1 2 3 4 5 6 7 8 9 10
Work with difficult/reluctant staff	0 1 2 3 4 5 6 7 8 9 10
Identify learning skills	0 1 2 3 4 5 6 7 8 9 10
Possess listening skills	0 1 2 3 4 5 6 7 8 9 10

Give feedback	0 1 2 3 4 5 6 7 8 9 10
Organise and prioritise objectives	0 1 2 3 4 5 6 7 8 9 10
Use Supervision Agreements	0 1 2 3 4 5 6 7 8 9 10
Establish and maintain boundaries	0 1 2 3 4 5 6 7 8 9 10
Identify and write clear supervision notes with goals	0 1 2 3 4 5 6 7 8 9 10
Understand the purpose and importance of supervision	0 1 2 3 4 5 6 7 8 9 10
Discuss issues of diversity and equality	0 1 2 3 4 5 6 7 8 9 10
Understand equal opportunities in supervision	0 1 2 3 4 5 6 7 8 9 10

APPENDICES

Appendix 1

SUPERVISION AGREEMENT

During the first supervision meeting a supervision agreement which sets out the parameters of supervision should be agreed and signed. The reason for this is to ensure that both supervisor and supervisee are aware of their roles and responsibilities in the supervision process.

The areas of contents could be:

- names of supervisor and supervisee

- length and frequency of the supervision meetings

- what each person can expect from each other, i.e. roles and responsibilities

- level of support required

- learning style

- supervision should be a two way process and both the supervisor and supervisee need to contribute to the supervision agenda

- confidentiality

- arrangements for recording, for example, if the supervision records are to be typed by someone other than the supervisor then the supervisor must get permission from the supervisee for this to happen, especially around issues of a personal or sensitive nature

- others who may have access to the supervision records, e.g. CQC Inspectors, Human Resources etc

- where and when supervisions will be held

- notice required for each supervision meeting

- if the supervisor is off for a long period which other supervisor will step in

- from time to time supervisors may change and the supervisee will be informed within one month of this happening

- what happens when supervision needs to be postponed, e.g. when an emergency arises

- areas at the bottom of the agreement for the supervisor and supervisee to sign and date. One copy should be kept by the supervisor and one by the supervisee

- who the supervisee should contact if they feel the terms of their supervision agreement are not being met.

You could design a form to incorporate two sections: one section listing the supervisor's responsibilities and one listing the supervisee's responsibilities.

It is advisable that you ask the employee you are going to supervise what their understanding of a supervision meeting is as it is important they know what it is and what their responsibilities are as a supervisee.

This supervision agreement should be reviewed by the supervisor and supervisee annually.

Both parties should agree to be bound by the written agreement.

Appendix 2

Personal Development Plan

Personal Development Plans (PDPs) are important working documents and will identify the employees training and development needs. They enable the employee and the supervisor to set objectives and goals and explore the best methods to achieve them. The supervisor will support the employees with these and it is a good way of tracking the employee's progress.

The Personal Development Plan is unique to the employee. It may have some similar goals to another colleague on it e.g. both employees need to know how to support an individual with his road skills then both employees Personal Development Plans will have this as an objective.

It should be used. It should not be put in a filing cabinet and never seen again.

Your organisation's Personal Development Plan may contain a few more columns. Here is an example of what it could look like:

What I need/want to learn	Why do I need to do it?	How will I do it?	When will I do it?	Review date

You can devise the personal development plan with the employee, set dates to achieve objectives and goals and review regularly.

It will have a front page and this page can contain the following:

Name:

Name of workplace:

Name of supervisor:

Goals:

Signed by staff member:
Date:

Signed by supervisor:
Date:

Date to be reviewed:

Appendix 3

BRIEF TO HELP YOU, THE SUPERVISOR GET THE MOST FROM SUPERVISION MEETINGS

What to do before the planned supervision

- Read through previous supervision notes
- Reflect on employees progress, achievements and performance in working towards and/or meeting objectives
- Think about any problems/obstacles that may affect performance, what can be put in place to reduce these, does the employee understand the policies and procedures, for example?
- Obtain feedback from colleagues (other managers and seniors)
- Start planning the agenda.

What to take with you

- previous supervision notes
- note pad and pen
- information on areas you wish to discuss
- information on the goals you will be setting
- job description (if supervising new employee for the first time)
- glass of water.

Supervision
Record

Setting the agenda

Supervision is a two way process and both the supervisee and supervisor must participate in making it an effective supervision meeting and one way to do this is for both people to make a list of what they would like to be discussed in the meeting.

You need to encourage supervisees to engage with supervision and take responsibility for working towards and meeting *their* goals. This will also include participating in setting the agenda. Some organisations encourage supervisors to have a standard agenda to ensure that the main areas are covered.

Areas on the standard agenda could be:

- Actions from last supervision meeting
- Health and Safety
- Reflection on incidents, risk assessments, work practices
- Key working
- Continuing professional development
- Refresher sessions on policies and procedures.

Sickness and well-being, such as

- How are you?
- Attendance (including sickness and absence)
- Annual leave/TOIL (time off in lieu)
- Time keeping.

Caseload/ workload generally, such as

- Are they getting the work done?
- Things they are doing well, things they are having difficulty with.
- Have they got too much or too little work?
- Do they have an awareness of the current or new policies or risk assessments?

Professional relationships, such as

- Do they have appropriate relationships with the people who use the service, staff, other?
- Are they team players and know how to work in a team and why they need to work in the team?
- What effect do they have on the dynamics within the team?

Overall employee performance

Other issues e.g. for managers/senior staff
- Budgets
- Business and/or strategic plans
- Complaints and investigations
- Recruitment and vacancies
- Staff performance and appraisals
- Staffing or rota issues
- Team progress.

Date and place of next supervision meeting.

Appendix 4

BRIEF TO HELP THE SUPERVISEE GET THE MOST FROM THEIR SUPERVISION MEETINGS

Before the supervision meeting:
- Have a look at the minutes of your last supervision. Is there anything that needs to be brought forward to your next supervision?
- Make a list of things you would like to discuss and get advice on.

Be prepared, take with you:
- Pen and paper
- Copy of last supervision minutes
- List of things you wish to discuss. Your supervisor will have their list too. At the beginning of the meeting you can both discuss your individual lists and put them onto one list which your supervisor can follow during the meeting
- Glass of water. You can ask your supervisor if s/he would like one too.

During the supervision meeting:
- Discuss action points from your last supervision
- Discuss areas of work
- Identify training needs
- Ask questions if you are unsure of anything
- Don't spend longer than is needed on each subject
- Try to keep to the subject you are talking about
- Set goals
- It is YOUR supervision, make the most of it!
- You will set a date for the next supervision that is convenient to you both.

After the supervision meeting:

- Implement any changes in work practice
- Start working towards achieving the goals.

Appendix 5

SUPERVISEE FEEDBACK FORM

My supervision-	Generally	Occasionally	Certainly not
Is regular			
Is private and uninterrupted			
Helps me to reflect on my work			
Helps me clarify my role and responsibilities			
Makes me aware of new or updated policies and procedures			
Identifies my training needs			
Enables me to discuss any issues or concerns I have			
Gives me positive and constructive feedback			
Is a two-way process			

Assists me in managing stress			
Is too long			
Is too short			
Is recorded on my Personal Development Plan			
I receive a written copy of my supervision			
The two areas in which I would most like supervision to improve are: 1. 2. 3. 4.			

Appendix 6

SUPERVISION FORM

Name of Supervisor:	
Name of Supervisee:	
Date of supervision:	

Agenda	Summary of discussions	Actions and timescale
Actions from last supervision meeting inc Key working		
Health and Safety e.g. Reflection on incidents, work practices		
Continuing professional development		
Sickness and well-being e.g. How are you? Attendance (including sickness and absence) Annual leave / time off in lieu Time keeping		

Refresher sessions on policies and procedures		
Service Users/residents		
Caseload/ workload generally e.g. Are they getting the work done? Things they are doing well, things they are having difficulty with. Have they got too much or too little work? Do they have an awareness of the current or new policies or risk assessments?		
Professional relationships e.g. Do they have appropriate relationships with the people who use the service, staff, other. Are they team players and know how to work in a team and why they need to work in the team? What effect do they have on the dynamics within the team?		

Overall employee performance		
Other issues e.g. for managers and senior staff Budgets Business and/or strategic plans Complaints and investigations Recruitment and vacancies Staff performance and appraisals Staffing or rota issues Team progress		
Date and place of next supervision meeting		

Signed by the Supervisor………………..…………….

Date …………………………..

Signed by the Supervisee …………………..………

Date …………………………

Copy to be given to employee, copy retained for managers records.

Supervision Skills

Appendix 7

SUPERVISION PROGRESS FORM

Date/ti me of supervi sion	Name of super visor	Name of supervisee	Tick when completed	If cancelled, state reason	Write alternative date	Signature of Supervisor	Signature of Supervisee

Appendix 8

CONTINUAL PROFESSIONAL DEVELOPMENT RECORD

Name...

Covering the period FROM:

.....................................to.....................................

....

Key dates	What did you do?	What did you learn by doing this?	How have you/or will you use what you have learnt?	Any further action

_____

Name of company

THIS IS TO CERTIFY THAT

_____

Name of learner

has completed training on

Supervision Skills

ON

_____

Date

Name of Manager/Trainer:

....

Signature of

Manager/Trainer...

Name of work place/training venue

....

Date.................................

This training has covered

Roles and responsibilities of supervisor and supervisee

What an induction and supervision is

The benefits of supervision

How to devise and prioritise an agenda

Provide equal opportunities

Equality and Diversity

Importance of supervisions

Frequency of supervision meetings

How to give feedback

Goals and objectives

Importance of a Personal Development Plan

Purpose of the Supervision Agreement and when and how to use it

How to identify different learning styles

How to listen effectively

The importance of confidentiality

Record keeping

Know how and where to seek advice

Manage poor performance

Useful Websites

All the following websites were accessed on 24th February 2015.

ACAS

http://www.acas.org.uk

Provides information for employers and employees.

Care Quality Commission

www.cqc.org.uk

The Care Quality Commission is the regulator of health and adult social care in England. They monitor services to ensure that the care people receive meets the essential standards of quality and safety.

Data Protection Act 1998

http://www.ico.gov.uk/for_organisations/data_protection.aspx

This Act protects the rights of the individual on information that is obtained, stored, processed or supplied and applies to both computerised and paper records and that appropriate security measures are in place.

Data Protection (Amendment) Act 2003

https://www.dataprotection.ie/documents/legal/act2003.pdf

Department of Health

www.dh.gov.uk

Providing health and social care policy, guidance and publications for NHS and social care professionals

Human Rights Act 1998

http://www.legislation.gov.uk/ukpga/1998/42/contents

This Act promotes the fundamental rights and freedoms contained in the European Convention on Human Rights.

Learn Direct

www.learndirect.co.uk

Learn Direct provide courses which are flexible and can be completed at home or work if you have access to the Internet or at a Learn Direct centre.

The new Care Certificate for support workers across social care and health in England

The Care Certificate will be implemented for all applicable new starters in health and social care from April 2015.

http://www.skillsforcare.org.uk/Standards/Care-Certificate/Care-Certificate.aspx

Skills for Care

www.skillsforcare.org.uk

Skills for Care helps people who do a great job do it better.

Skills Funding Agency

https://www.gov.uk/government/organisations/skills-funding-agency

Skills Funding Agency fund skills training for further education (FE) in England

References and Further Reading
REFERENCES

Active listening. http://en.wiktionary.org/wiki/active_listening
Brown, A. and Bourne, I. (1995) *The Social Work Supervisor. Supervision in community, day care and residential settings*, Buckingham: Open University Press.

(DoH 1993). Department of Health (1993) A vision for the future. Report of the Chief Nursing Officer.

David McClelland - Human Motivation Theory McClelland, D. C. (1961) *The achieving society*. Princeton: Van Nostrand.

Definition of Supervision.
http://www.definitions.net/definition/supervision

Honey, P. Learning Styles (Online), Available:
http://www.peterhoney.com/content/LearningStylesQuestionnaire. html (14th Aug 2014).

Kitwood T (1997) *Dementia reconsidered: the person comes first*. Berkshire, UK: Open University Press.
http://www.contemporarynurse.com/archives/vol/26/issue/2/artic le/590/person-centered-care

Kolb D.A. (1984) 'Experiential Learning experience as a source of learning and development', New Jersey: Prentice Hall

Mehrabian, A www.kaaj.com/psych

Reflective cycle, Gibbs 1988
http://www.health.uce.ac.uk/dpl/nursing/Placement%20Support/ Model%20of%20Reflection.htm

Strebler, M. Tackling Poor Performance (Report 4060, Brighton: Institute for Employment Studies, 2004 ISBN: 978-1-85184-339-8.

FURTHER READING

Alsop. A (2000). Continuing Professional Development: A Guide for Therapists. Blackwell Science, Oxford.

Christian, C. & Kitto, J. (1987) *The Theory and Practice of Supervision*, London: YMCA National College.

Parham. D. (1987). Towards Professionalism: The Reflective Therapist. Am. J. of O.T.

Schon. D. (1991). The Reflective Practitioner. How Professionals Think in Action. Jossey Barr, San Francisco.

About the author

Suzan Collins is an internationally selling author and writes in many styles and genres, fiction and non-fiction including textbooks that pertain to her work as a consultant and trainer in social care and management.

Non-Fiction:

Beyond My Control: Why the Health and Social Care System Need Not Have Failed My Mother was a People's Book Prize finalist and shortlisted for the Best Achievement Award.
ISBN: 978-1781610282

Making the Most of Your Supervision
ISBN: 978-0-9931690-2-1

<u>Coming soon:</u>

Safe Administration of Medication in Social Care
ISBN: 978-0-9931690-3-8

Medication: Assisting and Prompting
ISBN: 978-0-9931690-4-5

Suzan also writes fiction for adults and children. To find out more please visit her website: <u>www.suzancollins.com</u>

NOTES

NOTES

11684359R10073

Printed in Great Britain
by Amazon.co.uk, Ltd.,
Marston Gate.